Colours All Around Us

Green

Daniel Nunn

Raintree

www.raintreepublishers.co.uk
Visit our website to find out
more information about
Raintree books.

To order:
☎ Phone 0845 6044371
📠 Fax +44 (0) 1865 312263
📧 Email myorders@raintreepublishers.co.uk

Customers from outside the UK please telephone +44 1865 312262

Raintree is an imprint of Capstone Global Library Limited, a company incorporated in England and Wales having its registered office at 7 Pilgrim Street, London, EC4V 6LB – Registered company number: 6695582

Text © Capstone Global Library Limited 2012
First published in hardback in 2012
The moral rights of the proprietor have been asserted.

Edited by Dan Nunn, Rebecca Rissman, and Catherine Veitch
Designed by Joanna Hinton-Malivoire
Picture research by Ruth Blair
Originated by Capstone Global Library Ltd.
Production by Victoria Fitzgerald
Printed in China by South China Printing Company Ltd

ISBN 978 1 406 22597 6
15 14 13 12 11
10 9 8 7 6 5 4 3 2 1

British Library Cataloguing in Publication Data
Nunn, Daniel.
Green. – (Colours All Around Us)
535.6-dc22

Acknowledgements
We would like to thank the following for permission to reproduce photographs: Shutterstock pp. 4 (© tlorna), 5 (© stavklem, © cloki, © Anastasia Bobrova, © Chris Lishman, © mojito.mak[dog]gmail[dot]com, © Strakovskaya, © Anna Sedneva), 6 (© Martin Valigursky), 7 (© Elnur), 9 (© Four Oaks), 10 (© M.antonis), 11 (© dabjola), 12 L (© wildlywise), 12 R (© Nikita Chisnikov), 13 (© matka Wariatka), 14 (© Bedolaga, © Martin Capek, © Tamara Kulikova), 15 (© Leonid and Anna Dedukh), 16 (© Gorilla), 17 (© Anna Jurkovska), 19 (© Zurijeta), 21 (© Monkey Business Images), 22 L (© elenadesign), 22 R (© calldanai), 23 (© odze, © kret87, © tratong, © stavklem).

Front cover photograph of a tree frog reproduced with permission of Shutterstock (© Brberrys). Back cover photographs reproduced with permission of Shutterstock (© cloki, © stavklem, © Anna Sedneva, © kret87).

Every effort has been made to contact copyright holders of any material reproduced in this book. Any omissions will be rectified in subsequent printings if notice is given to the publisher.

Disclaimer
All the Internet addresses (URLs) given in this book were valid at the time of going to press. However, due to the dynamic nature of the Internet, some addresses may have changed, or sites may have changed or ceased to exist since publication. While the author and publisher regret any inconvenience this may cause readers, no responsibility for any such changes can be accepted by either the author or the publisher.

Contents

Green all around us

Let's look for colours!
It's time to play!

How many green things
can you find today?

Let's go to the zoo

Oh what fun! A trip to the zoo!

We can see green frogs and green parrots, too!

SQUAWK!

Look over there!

Sliding through the grass!

A green snake hisses
as it slithers past.

And what's this here?

Crawling ever so **slow**?

It's a tiny green caterpillar.

Go caterpillar, go!

A green lunch

Let's have some lunch.
Is any food green?

You could try eating broccoli!
Or perhaps a green bean?

Try a green pudding
and eat something sweet.

Green apples, green pears,
or green grapes are a treat.

Play time!

Let's go to the park.
We can play hide-and-seek!

Quick, hide behind this green bush,
I promise not to peek!

16

1 2 3 Coming ready or not!

My turn! I think I'll hide behind this green tree.

You can look all you like, but you won't find me!

Home time

Haven't we had fun, playing
in this green park?

But we'd better go home now,
before it gets dark!

What else is green?

It has been a busy day!

Can you think of anything else that is green?

23

Colour challenge

Can you find a green animal sliding through the grass?

Index

24